FOOTBALL HALL OF FAMERS

FRAN TARKENTON

David Hulm

the rosen publishing group's
rosen
central

Published in 2003 by The Rosen Publishing Group, Inc.
29 East 21st Street, New York, NY 10010

First Edition

Library of Congress Cataloging-in-Publication Data

Hulm, David.
Fran Tarkenton / David Hulm.— 1st ed.
    p. cm. — (Football Hall of Famers)
Summary: Outlines the life and victories of Minnesota
Vikings and New York Giants football legend Fran
Tarkenton, who became a successful businessman at the
end of his football career.
Includes bibliographical references and index.
ISBN 0-8239-3608-2 (lib. bdg.)
1. Tarkenton, Fran—Juvenile literature. 2. Football
players—United States—Biography—Juvenile literature.
[1. Tarkenton, Fran. 2. Football players.]
I. Title. II. Series.
GV939.T3 H85 2003
796.332'092—dc21

                                                    2002001636

Manufactured in the United States of America

Contents

Fran Tarkenton, one of the best quarterbacks in NFL history, was noted for his ability to run with the ball while looking for a receiver. He set numerous NFL passing records during his career with the Minnesota Vikings and New York Giants. He was elected to the Pro Football Hall of Fame in 1986.

Introduction

Fran Tarkenton may not be a household name today, but he is still considered one of the National Football League's (NFL) greatest quarterbacks. Until 1995, he held NFL lifetime records for most pass completions (3,686), most yards gained passing (47,003), and most touchdown passes (342) during his career with the Minnesota Vikings (1961–1966, 1972–1978) and the New York Giants (1967–1971).

As a rookie quarterback in his first professional game, Fran Tarkenton came off the Minnesota Vikings bench, threw four touchdowns, and ran for one touchdown. If passer ratings (the mathematical formula used to grade a quarterback's efficiency) were in effect at the time, his would have been over

148 (150 is a perfect rating). It was September 17, 1961, and the first victory for the brand-new Vikings. What began on that day for Tarkenton continued for sixteen seasons. The Vikings suffered critical losses with Tarkenton at the helm, including three Super Bowl defeats. But more often than not, Tarkenton was one of the most exciting quarterbacks to watch during football season.

Tarkenton's place in NFL history is quite secure. He will forever be known as Scramblin' Fran because of the way he scrambled behind the line of scrimmage. When pass rushers attacked, Tarkenton developed an elusive style that took him from sideline to sideline, sometimes wearing down the rushers, sometimes wearing down his receivers and their defenders.

Hall of Fame linebacker Ted Hendricks describes Tarkenton's abilities this way in an interview for *Sports Illustrated*'s Web site: "The one [quarterback] that was the hardest to catch was Fran Tarkenton. He ran back and forth across the field and I think the best you could do was to stop and wait for him to come back to you again." Tarkenton was famous for creating frustration and desperation in opponents' defenses as he moved across the field, sometimes ducking into his own end zone to launch a pass that would end up, miraculously, in his receiver's hands.

Deacon Jones, a Hall of Fame defensive end, had great respect for Tarkenton, but also severe loathing reserved only for formidable opponents. "He had eyes in the back of his head. I'm thoroughly convinced of that," Jones said in an interview for NFL Films. "You could approach him from the rear and he's looking downfield, but he feels you and sees you. And he would react."

Tarkenton's ability to react was something that drove both the defenses he faced and his own coaches crazy. He broke all the rules. Normally, society does not praise individuals for breaking rules. Often, when we hear about professional athletes who break rules, the incidents involve the police, arrests, and trials. The only trials in Tarkenton's case were on the field.

For nearly two decades, Tarkenton's ability to get the ball close to his receivers and in the end zone topped the record books. "The guy was exciting," Jones says in NFL's *Greatest Moments*. "He was great for the game. And I thought that after Fran Tarkenton displayed his skills in the league, that this league would finally understand how devastating a moving quarterback could be."

Another Hall of Famer, former Minnesota Vikings head coach Bud Grant, says in the same film that Tarkenton was much more than a scrambler. "Fran was only 5 foot 10 and a half—he might tell you he's bigger, but he's not—he weighed about 178 pounds—he might tell you he's 185, but he's not. He would move to find the gaps to throw between people to hit the receivers." Grant calls Tarkenton the most competitive person he knew, someone who "couldn't wait for Sundays." For 16 consecutive seasons, Fran Tarkenton amazed and rattled professional football players, coaches, and fans.

And although Tarkenton virtually invented the running quarterback position, it was not a conscious decision. Previously, quarterbacks

From the beginning of his professional career Fran Tarkenton used his ability to scramble, or elude tacklers and rush for yardage, which became his trademark. Here he rolls out of the pocket during a Vikings game.

were coached to stay in the pocket and take the sack. This caused numerous injuries and enormous losses in yards. Although it's hard to believe now, this was the way it was done.

Because the Vikings were a young franchise comprised of other teams' cast-offs and rookie draftees, their offensive schemes didn't quite click. Tarkenton could not always read the defense clearly, nor could he predict where his receivers were going. But he had patience, desire, and talent, which developed over the course of his career. He could also run, and that's what he did until he could find someone to connect with his passes. He wasn't just running away to avoid the physical pain of getting tackled. He ran to find success.

Tarkenton led the Vikings to three Super Bowls (VIII, IX, and XI). He was an All-NFL selection four times, and he played in nine Pro Bowls. In 1986, he became the first Minnesota Viking elected to the Pro Football Hall of Fame.

Tarkenton found success. And he continues to find success. Today, he is well known for his business leadership and inspirational speeches.

He is a consultant to numerous Fortune 500 companies, and his own companies, the Fran Tarkenton Small Business NETwork, Tarkenton NETwork, and Tarkenton Net Ventures, have annual revenues ranging up to $142 million.

What Tarkenton says now about business is what he has said since his beginnings as a high school athlete and what he writes on his Web site, www.tarkenton.com: "We have to have a passion for what we are doing. Whatever you are involved in today, if you don't have passion, don't do it." In his many speeches, he emphasizes how important teamwork is to success. Individuals do not win, whether in sports or business—teams do. Fran Tarkenton is one of those rare people who helps others become winners.

From the Sandlots to Sound Fundamentals

Francis Asbury Tarkenton was born in 1940 in Richmond, Virginia, and lived there for five years. His father, Dallas, was an evangelical preacher and instilled a strong religious faith in young Fran. After Sunday services, Fran, his brother, and his father would play ball inside or outside their home. His love of sports began then.

Tarkenton developed his scrambling abilities in a narrow alley in Washington, D.C., where the family moved next. Because there wasn't much room to play, the neighborhood boys had to learn to use the space as best they could. Tarkenton developed his instincts for evasion and direction at an early age.

Another source of inspiration for Tarkenton was his brother, Dallas Jr. Dallas was older,

Tarkenton grew up in the nation's capital, Washington D.C. It was during that time he learned how to scramble and hustle playing in the narrow backstreets of the city.

stronger, and faster than Fran. Like many younger brothers, Fran sought the company of his older brother. This meant he would often play with boys who were three and four years older. Tarkenton already had a keen sense of competition, and competing with more experienced boys only fueled his determination to become better.

On rainy days, Tarkenton would arrange his collection of football cards into teams. He would study player statistics and create ultimate football teams of equal strength. His serious study of football cards made him even more curious about the rules and strategies of the game. When he got older, he would eventually face some of the men whose cards he had collected. As he writes in his autobiography, *No Time for Losing*, "I think I knew as much about them as they knew about themselves."

The Importance of Dedication

"I don't know how I could have been programmed better for a high school career," Tarkenton writes in a later autobiography,

Tarkenton, cowritten by Jim Klobuchar. "By the time my family left Washington, D.C., and came to Athens [Georgia] where my daddy was going to preach, I had decided without equivocation [without a doubt] that I was going to be a professional athlete. I fantasized with bubble-gum pictures in the attic, and I fantasized in the sandlots. I played all the time."

That seriousness helped Tarkenton develop a dedication to a sport, which he feels should begin at an early age. Young players have the luxury of being able to risk failure and to experiment and try new things. Because most young athletes do not have to worry about being booed, they should not be discouraged by a lack of skill. When you are young, Tarkenton feels, you should only be obsessed by your love of playing the game.

While in high school in Georgia, Tarkenton made it to the varsity team. Of his early successes and failures, Tarkenton writes in *No Time For Losing*: "It was a case, really, of perhaps a less talented player (myself) going further in the long run because my desires were channeled more purposefully. My determination and tremendous desire to be as good an athlete as possible demanded practice and concentration and eventually resulted in the abilities I have today."

His high school coach, Weyman Sellers, also helped in this regard. Sellers's reputation for toughness kept Tarkenton in excellent physical shape. Tarkenton notes in *Tarkenton*, "When I was introduced to the Dutchman's [Norm Van Brocklin, head coach of the Minnesota Vikings] two-a-day drills at the Viking's camp in Bemidji, everybody seemed appalled. They could never figure out why I was so calm about it. Actually I was grateful. If Sellers ran the Vikings he would have scheduled a third one at night. But he taught me the fundamentals of playing quarterback, the techniques that stood up the rest of my career."

Tarkenton's philosophy for playing sports was quite simple and very realistic: "I realized that no matter how hard I might play to win, there will inevitably be some losses, and I had better be prepared to take them without bitterness or discouragement." It was a philosophy

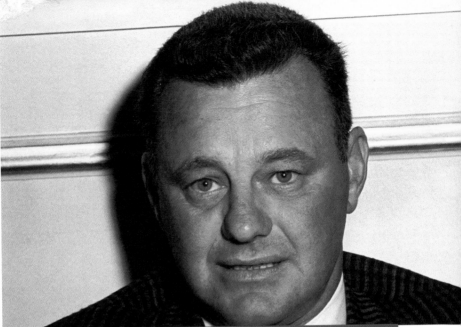

Norm Van Brocklin, head coach of the Minnesota Vikings. It was Van Brocklin's tough love that spurred Tarkenton to many a memorable performance. As a player, Van Brocklin led the NFL in passing three times and punting twice. He also won two NFL titles and an MVP award.

that led Tarkenton to college championships and three Super Bowls.

Preparing for the Future

In addition to football, Tarkenton participated in baseball, tennis, and basketball. He served as a class officer, and had many other extracurricular activities. Through all of this activity, he maintained a high academic standard. How did he do it? In *No Time for Losing*, he writes, "I knew the importance of good grades—especially if I wanted a scholarship to college—I simply made the time [to study] whenever possible."

Tarkenton did not resent the time he took to study, as he recognized the importance of a solid education for his future: "I found time for the sports I loved and for the studying I needed—and I was determined to stick with it and win in whatever I had to do."

In high school, Tarkenton was faced with the same challenges and distractions most people face. His devotion to God, building his own character, and a desire for sincerity kept him away from activities that he felt were questionable or harmful.

In his junior year, Tarkenton helped lead his team to a perfect record and a state championship. Their victory helped elevate them to a higher classification and a tougher set of opponents. The next season, it didn't help that many of the other stars on the championship team had graduated.

In his senior year, Tarkenton and his high school team experienced repeated failure. He did not, however, focus on the negative aspects of the losing record. "When you consider what we had to work with, I think it [a 4-6 record] was a miracle," he writes in *No Time for Losing*. But as talented and successful as he had been, Tarkenton did not see his future in football. He was much more in love with the game of baseball.

Fran Tarkenton saw himself as a "natural" baseball player. As a pitcher he'd had numerous shutouts; as a shortstop, he'd made brilliant defensive plays. In the late 1950s, baseball was much more popular than football in the United States, and Tarkenton had attracted the attention of a professional scout. But a lingering injury in his throwing arm would prevent him from achieving that dream. Luckily, it didn't affect his quarterbacking skills. In fact, he describes the injury as a blessing in disguise because it allowed him to focus more on football.

Nearly 40 colleges offered scholarships to Tarkenton, and selecting the right school was not an easy task. He narrowed his choices to three, and the University of Georgia was

Tarkenton *(left)* poses with a University of Georgia coach and another teammate in this photo. Tarkenton was an all-state quarterback in high school and an All-American at the University of Georgia.

ranked third on his list. Even though he'd heard that Wally Butts, the head coach at Georgia, was very tough and that two other freshmen were in competition for the second and third quarterback positions, Tarkenton accepted the offer and the challenge. He had consulted his father, who asked if Fran had prayed on the matter. Tarkenton followed his father's advice and prayed, but he did not get any kind of thunder-and-lightning answer. Instead, he felt a kind of confidence that he was being guided in the direction of the University of Georgia.

Another benefit of the University of Georgia was that it was close enough for Tarkenton to live at home in the off-season. He would still be surrounded by the comfort of his family, whom he greatly valued. Tarkenton's mother, Frances, had always been supportive of her son's activities. She was a great football fan and provided helpful nurturing from the beginning. His father was not as interested in the game itself, but he always kept his children's goals close to his heart and in his prayers. Tarkenton would need the support of his family in the difficult years to come.

Most
Fortunate
Among Men

At the University of Georgia, Tarkenton became captain of the freshmen team. His father served as team chaplain. Tarkenton writes in *No Time for Losing* that before a crucial game with Georgia Tech, his father offered this "sermon" to the team: "Fellows, I got me a yellow jacket today. And now if each of you will go out there today and get yourself a Yellowjacket [the team name for the Georgia Tech freshmen squad], we'll go home the winners." Forty thousand fans attended the game, which ended in victory for the University of Georgia. Tarkenton credits his father's ability to relieve the players' tension and raise their already heightened spirits.

Tarkenton remembers assistant coach Quinton Lumpkin with great fondness. "The guy who really got me ready psychologically and technically for college football was Quinton Lumpkin. He had been a great center at Georgia," Tarkenton writes in *Tarkenton.* "He was the kind who lived in the dormitory with players, a principled, hard-fibered, decent guy who was a man among men. Nobody ever challenged Quinton Lumpkin."

Tarkenton was blessed with a coach who believed in his players and in the system. Winning was just one of the benefits of learning from Coach Lumpkin. According to Tarkenton, the coach was someone "you could confide in if things got rough." For that first season of college football, little got rough. Tarkenton's team won all their games, including a preseason matchup with the varsity team.

Football was not the only thing going well in Tarkenton's life. In addition to making lifelong friends with several players on his team, Tarkenton also started dating his future wife, Elaine Merrill, during his freshman year at the University of Georgia.

Despite a shaky start, Tarkenton emerged as a star quarterback at the University of Georgia and went on to become one of the first successful running quarterbacks in NFL history.

Overcoming Obstacles

In *No Time for Losing*, Tarkenton describes his sophomore year as being his "strangest season." At the beginning of the season, it looked like he was going to sit on the bench as the third-string quarterback. Coach Butts had other quarterbacks, all talented, whom he decided would play first, despite Tarkenton's past accomplishments. And rumor had it Butts wouldn't even consider playing sophomore quarterbacks. Despite the odds, Tarkenton was certain that he would be Georgia's quarterback.

During their first game, Georgia was down 7–0 against Texas and hadn't even managed a first down in the first half. In the third quarter, Butts finally gave in to Tarkenton's pleading and brought him in. Tarkenton assured his coach that he would get a touchdown for the team.

The drive began on the five-yard line, and Tarkenton took his offense to the end zone, scoring a touchdown. They were successful with a two-point pass conversion. Georgia was now ahead. After Texas scored again, Tarkenton was surprised when Coach Butts put in Charlie

Britt as quarterback. Although he was bigger and stronger, Britt could not lead the team to success. Georgia lost. Tarkenton was upset, and a little angry, too.

"The number of nonbelievers in Francis Tarkenton in football has been very impressive, and you might even say scary," he writes in *Tarkenton*. To be fair, Butts had no reason to believe Tarkenton was any better than the other quarterbacks. Tarkenton would strive to make Butts a believer, but first he would have to overcome a few major obstacles.

Despite Tarkenton's brief success in the game against Texas, it became clear that Coach Butts would only use him when it suited his game plan. University of Georgia fans thought that Tarkenton had been unfairly treated, being removed from a game that they thought he could win. To their delight, Tarkenton was chosen as starting quarterback for the next game. After a three-and-out beginning series, Tarkenton was yanked, Charlie Britt came in, and Tarkenton did not see any more playing time that game. Georgia lost.

During the next few games, Tarkenton played only sporadically, and his level of play reflected the unstable nature of his position on the team. Then Tarkenton got a dose of reality and an earful from his coach. After a particularly poor game performance, Tarkenton heard language that, as a preacher's son, he was not used to hearing. Coach Butts, who had a reputation for tough talking, cut into Tarkenton at practice like he was a side of beef. The future scrambler was appalled, and later wrote in *Tarkenton*: "This was the first time it happened to me, and it wasn't going to happen again. I was finished with Georgia, and I walked off the field."

Players often hear offensive language both on and off the field, but Tarkenton felt Coach Butts's lashing had been extreme. He told his coach that he was not coming back and he and two other players planned to go to Florida State.

The next day, Coach Lumpkin visited the players in their dorm. In his quiet and unassuming way, Lumpkin convinced the players that what they had experienced was simply the way the practice field was, and that they should never take it personally. Because of their trust in Lumpkin as a man, they went back. They also felt their teammates needed them, and they were bound by a sense of loyalty.

Eventually, Tarkenton played quarterback when the team was on the offensive—when they absolutely had to score points. When the team was in a defensive position, protecting a lead, Britt was the quarterback.

At the end of the season, Tarkenton was selected quarterback on the All-Southeastern Conference team. Tarkenton felt that his skills as a football player had improved under the guidance of Coach Butts. In fact, in *No Time for Losing*, Tarkenton refers to Butts as "the finest coach in football."

Gaining Momentum

During his junior season in 1959, Tarkenton acquired a nickname. One member of the press referred to him as the "Praying Passer." Though Tarkenton does not believe God takes sides in football games, he found strength and calmness through prayer. He needed both of

Tarkenton led the University of Georgia to a resounding win in the Orange Bowl in 1960, bagging the MVP award for himself in the process.

those qualities several times during that season, no more so than when Georgia played Auburn for the right to go to the Orange Bowl.

Late in the game, with the score tied at 7–7, Georgia was trapped deep in their own territory and was forced to punt. Bobby Walden, the Georgia punter, botched the kick. The ball bounced right into the back of Charlie Britt, and Auburn recovered the ball on the one-yard line. Auburn scored, making their lead 13–7, and then missed the extra point. With a minute and a half left in the game, Auburn fumbled, giving Georgia possession at the Auburn 45-yard line. Tarkenton came in and threw three incomplete passes. On fourth and ten, he connected, leading Georgia down to the Auburn seven. Three plays later, after a sack left them at fourth down, 13 yards to go, Tarkenton called time-out.

Instead of checking with Coach Butts at the sidelines, Tarkenton drew up the play in the huddle, just as he had when he fantasized about such moments as a child. He concocted a timing pattern to his left end, with misdirection to the right. The rollout pattern to the right worked well. The defense bought it. The fans bought it. Tarkenton threw the ball across the field, and Bill Herron, the receiver, was wide open. Touchdown. "I almost never call plays like that," he writes in *Tarkenton*. "And I don't usually admit when I do." Durwood Pennington, the kicker, came in and, without the slightest hesitation, kicked the game-winning extra point. When the stadium was empty and quiet, Tarkenton took time to thank God for giving him the confidence and poise in what was, up to that point in his career, one of his most important moments in football.

In the victory over Auburn, Tarkenton had once again broken the rules. But in this case the "penalty" was a trip to the Orange Bowl on New Years Day, 1960. On the strength of excellent defense and two touchdown passes by Tarkenton, Georgia beat Missouri 14–0. Tarkenton was named Most Valuable Player for offensive quarterback, and Wally Butts won the United Press International award as SEC (South Eastern Conference) Coach of the Year.

Tarkenton continued to win critical college games, just as he would win pro games in the years to come. But before his NFL career began, there were some significant changes in his life. He became engaged to Elaine, and married her in December 1960. He also changed his major in college to business administration. This would ultimately become one of the most important decisions Tarkenton would ever make, one that would add to his growing legend as a breaker of rules.

Tarkenton walks off the field with his fiancée, Elaine Merrill, after a University of Georgia game in 1960.

His final season of college football, however, would present its own challenges. J.B. Whitworth, a defensive coach for Georgia, died of a heart attack just before the team's spring practices. Despite the tragic loss of Whitworth and the fact that Charlie Britt had graduated, Tarkenton felt that the Georgia team had all the necessary components to repeat the success of the championship. In fact, he thought they could be even better than the previous year's team.

After losing their opening game with Alabama, Tarkenton played in his most tiring game to date, a win over Vanderbilt, 18–7. He spent most of his time getting hammered into the ground, and he collapsed in the shower room after the game. The team then went on to win four games, then lost one more and went to Florida with a 5-2 record. Before the game, Tarkenton suffered an asthma attack, brought on by some unknown allergy. Usually these attacks required some time off, but being a competitor he decided to play while on medication.

On a scoring drive, Tarkenton kept the ball and dove for the end zone. He scored a touchdown but passed out and had to be carried off the field. Even more critical, he was hit on the hip during that play. The injury would dog him for the next couple of games. Somehow, Tarkenton returned to the field, completing 24 of 28 passes. Despite his heroic efforts, Georgia lost to Florida 22–14.

Tarkenton was so wrapped up and bandaged for the next game against Auburn that he was immobile in the pocket. Georgia won the close game, 9–6. In what was supposed to be his final game at the University of Georgia, he faced arch rivals Georgia Tech. Exuberance, melancholy, and sadness were all part of the emotional backdrop for a game that would be decided by a blocked extra point—in the University of Georgia's favor. Tarkenton's career playing for Georgia was over. It had been a satisfying journey.

Even more satisfying for him was his marriage to Elaine. With numerous awards received that year, his studies, and his new bride, Tarkenton writes in *No Time for Losing*, "I was indeed among the most fortunate of men."

In the Wilds
of Minnesota

Fran Tarkenton fully expected to be drafted in the first round of the 1961 draft. He had performed extremely well in his college career, earning honors and helping his team win a national title. In fact, he thought he would have his pick of teams. The commissioner of professional football told him numerous teams were interested in him.

At that time, professional football was made up of two conferences—the NFL and the AFL (American Football League). Players were drafted by both conferences, and the players decided the team they would play for. Their decisions were motivated by the size of the contract, the strength of the league (the NFL was more established; the AFL was considered

American Football League Commissioner Joe Foss in 1964, after announcing a deal between the AFL and NBC to televise AFL games. The AFL only existed for 10 years, but before it folded it managed to transform pro football, bring more fans in, help create the Super Bowl, and increase television coverage. In the process, it gave the NFL a run for its money.

weaker), and player preferences for teams. Tarkenton wanted to play for the NFL, and he wanted a team that would use his talents.

The Boston Patriots (now the New England Patriots) of the AFL and a new franchise in the NFL, the Minnesota Vikings, both drafted Tarkenton. He was disappointed because he wasn't taken until the third round. He had always believed that all great quarterbacks were drafted in the first round. What Tarkenton forgot is that many great and future Hall of Fame quarterbacks were not, and still are not, drafted in the first round. In *No Time for Losing* he writes, "It didn't help my feelings any to be a third choice and it just challenged me even more to go with the Vikings and prove to everyone that I could play with the big boys in the NFL."

Among those big boys was George Shaw, the starting quarterback brought into Minnesota from the New York Giants. Head coach Norm "The Dutchman" Van Brocklin planned to play Tarkenton only when victory was already assured, or when the Vikings were so far behind

Tarkenton was a passionate player who was upset by bad performances. Here he looks on angrily during a game in which the Los Angeles Rams scored three touchdowns and a field goal in the second half to beat the Vikings 34–10.

that developing their young quarterback would be more useful to the team than trying to win an unwinnable game.

The brand-new Minnesota Vikings were building a team from the ground up, and many of the players on that first Vikings team had known what it was like to be beaten into the ground. They were outcasts from various teams, seasoned veterans who were looking at the tail end of a career, or young rookies eager to get a break and make names for themselves in the wilds of Minnesota.

Jim Klobuchar, now a close friend of Tarkenton and someone who has chronicled Tarkenton's career extensively, writes in *Tarkenton*, "In their original trappings the Vikings were not so much a team as a loosely maintained wildlife preserve."

Coach Van Brocklin, who had just finished his own professional playing career, wanted to be well liked and to let the team have fun. But he also wanted to win. He soon learned he could not have it both ways. Discipline became his trademark, and physical exhaustion was the tool he used to fashion these cast-offs into a respectable football team. He discovered the value of creating team leaders—choosing players who could by example help him develop the motley assortment into a winning team. Loyalty would come slowly. The Dutchman could be quite sharp with his words, lashing out at veteran and rookie alike. In *Tarkenton*, the former quarterback remembers Van Brocklin telling him, "If you could throw, you'd be a real menace."

Rookie on the Bench

Tarkenton was not used to sitting on the bench. But being overlooked was a problem he had faced before, and he would approach the problem the same way he had in the past—with determination and vision. However, determination only goes so far, and as Tarkenton would learn, the NFL is quite different from high school and college football. If he thought college football was physical, the beatings he took in meaningless pro exhibition games were a brutal wake-up call.

Norm Van Brocklin during his days playing for the Los Angeles Rams. He led the Rams to an NFL title victory in 1951 and repeated the feat with the Philadelphia Eagles in 1960, when he also won an MVP award.

He describes in *Tarkenton* what happened after the Vikings fourth preseason game against the Chicago Bears: "I can't even remember what the score was, or anything about the game, except when I came back to Minneapolis, Elaine met me at the door and she could hardly recognize me. My legs were swollen, I had cuts on my face, and I looked and felt as if the whole Bear team had used me as the football."

In the Vikings' last preseason game, against the Los Angeles Rams, Tarkenton finally felt a level of success. As he remembers in *No Time for Losing*, the Vikings were trailing by 21 points, and he was sent in. He led the team to 17 points. "On that afternoon, I started becoming a professional quarterback. It had taken a lot of bruises and some painful experiences to bring it about, but I knew now that I was on the way." It was not a victory in the win-loss column, but it was a moral victory for the young quarterback, who was now known as P.K., the Preacher's Kid.

Fran Tarkenton clearly saw skill and victory as important goals of playing football. But even more important, he never forgot how much fun he had playing the game. He had loved it as a boy, and he still loved it now, as his job.

Facing the Bears in the 1961 season opener, Coach Van Brocklin chose experience over raw talent by starting Shaw instead of Tarkenton. The Bears were playing horribly, giving Minnesota every opportunity to rip the game wide open, but the Vikings did not make use of the Bears' weaknesses. Finally, Van Brocklin sent in Tarkenton. In less than five minutes, Tarkenton threw the first of four touchdown passes and ran another in for a touchdown. It appeared as though a leader had emerged.

Not quite. The Vikings followed the phenomenal success of the first game with seven straight, humiliating losses. Tarkenton saw little playing time during this run, except as a holder for extra points and field goals. But this was not an unusual start for a rookie quarterback. Most pro quarterbacks do not start during their rookie seasons and many ride the bench for two, even three years before they get their days in the sun, and the mud, and the snow.

To say that Shaw's abilities disappointed Van Brocklin would be an understatement. Finally, in disgust, he put Tarkenton in as the starting quarterback. The Preacher's Kid would need all of his childhood fantasies, college experience, faith, and spectator wisdom to redefine the role of a professional quarterback. His learning curve would earn him both praise and ridicule.

Scramblin' Fran

Tarkenton had watched other quarterbacks stay in the pocket and get hammered by the defense. To him, they were accepting defeat. That was not his game. "I wasn't setting myself up as a trailblazer," he told Jim Klobuchar in *Tarkenton*. "You do what you can to win. In my early years with the Vikings the only way I saw open to keep a drive alive, or to salvage a play where the blocking broke down, was to turn it into a helter-skelter situation where instincts and adlibbing gave you a chance . . . I started with an expansion team, and I used what was available to me— my quickness, reaction time, sandlot intuition, I

George Shaw, the number-one NFL draft pick in 1955, was an All-American from Oregon. After playing with the Baltimore Colts and the New York Giants, he joined the Minnesota Vikings. He failed to live up to his promise, however, and would retire in 1962. The 1955 draft is also notable as the year that the legendary Johnny Unitas made his debut—as a ninth-round pick and 102nd overall.

don't really care what you call it. Sometimes it worked, sometimes not."

When it did work, Tarkenton was brilliant. If you watch highlight reels from NFL films of Tarkenton, you will see where the modern quarterback began—in the fleet foot and fantastic arm of Scramblin' Fran Tarkenton. When it did not work, you will see sheer desperation and panic on Tarkenton's face. "We had some colossal boomerangs, of course. I set a still-standing record by fumbling into a forty-five-yard loss against the Rams," he says in *Tarkenton*. In that same game, however, he set a quarterback record of 99 yards rushing, a team record that would stand for nearly 40 years.

Twisting and turning in the face of logic and defensive ends, Tarkenton created a reputation as a fierce competitor, a giant in adversity, and a legend in Minnesota. In November 2000, Daunte Culpepper set a new Vikings team record for most rushing yards by a quarterback in a season, breaking the record Tarkenton set in 1966. As fewer games were played each season in 1966, one can imagine how impressive Tarkenton was on the

Daunte Culpepper, who joined the Minnesota Vikings in 1999, has lived up to the impressive standards Tarkenton set.

field. "He's a legend," Culpepper said of Tarkenton on *Sports Illustrated*'s Web site. "It's great to be a part of the tradition."

John Donovan writes on the same site, "The best of the smaller QBs was probably Tarkenton, who retired as the league's most prolific [productive] passer, with more than 47,000 yards in his career. Tarkenton was the consummate scrambler, running for more than 3,600 yards (and an average of 5.4 yards a carry) in his 18-year career with the Minnesota Vikings and New York Giants."

In a characteristic rushing play Fran Tarkenton *(number 10)* charges across the goal line for a third-quarter touchdown against the Chicago Bears in a 1973 game that Minnesota won 31–12.

"Fran was not big, but he was a great movement guy, with a very quick delivery, and smart," Eddie LeBaron, former quarterback of the Dallas Cowboys, said on *Sports Illustrated*'s

No Diagram for a Scramble

A dmirers of the modern-day Tarkenton may not grasp the magnitude of some of the odysseys of his youth. He was the Magellan of pro football. Visiting scouts assigned to chart the Vikings offense would be on their third box of tranquilizers by the second quarter. There was no known system for diagramming a Tarkenton scramble. The defensive ends would pinch on him, and Tarkenton would pivot and flee, bound for one sideline or other but occasionally his own end zone. By the time he had retreated thirty yards, his location had been fixed by most of the defensive team but not always by Van Brocklin. Crossfield the herd would come, pounding and snorting while Tarkenton, large-eyed but usually under control, would calculate the exact moment when he had to change course to avert decapitation.

—Jim Klobuchar in *Tarkenton*

Web site. "Balls didn't get knocked down because he had the ability to run around and find an open receiver. If you can make a guy miss a time or two, all sorts of options open up."

For the 1961 season, the Vikings managed few wins, but Tarkenton finished second in Rookie of the Year voting. He established an NFL record for most consecutive passes completed, with 13 in the 42–21 win over the Rams. He threw for nearly 2,000 yards and 18 touchdown passes. Of that first season, Tarkenton recalls in *Tarkenton*, "There was a lot of snickering about the quality of the Vikings castoffs, but I'll always respect those guys. They had no reason to be loyal to the Minnesota Vikings as such, and no responsibility . . . to build any kind of togetherness. But they did. They integrated the kids with the vets. They organized parties, established traditions that are still with the team."

The Vikings
Take Off

Often, statistics and accounts of major victories summarize a football player's career. Fans are concerned with the team's record, division or conference championships, Super Bowl visits, and Pro Bowl representation.

Football players, however, see their careers differently. Yes, they review the season and particular games. They recall fierce competitors or significant plays. But it is not the statistics that matter most. What they remember forever are the people they played the game with and the coaches who helped shape their careers. Head coach Norm Van Brocklin will be remembered by all who worked with him. He shaped the traditions of the Vikings as a leading NFL franchise.

A Strong Mental Attitude

The second season for the Minnesota Vikings yielded only two victories. This lack of success certainly caused stress for Tarkenton, who was used to winning games, seasons, and championships. His relationship with his head coach, the Dutchman, was also strained. Van Brocklin continued to berate Tarkenton.

When coming from a person one respects, harsh words are often hard to take, even if you are a tough NFL quarterback, or any other player on the roster, for that matter. Those comments confuse players, who often take it personally, instead of realizing the coach may just be venting frustration. Most of the time, Tarkenton took Van Brocklin's words with a grain of salt. He could see how much the Vikings success meant to Van Brocklin, and Van Brocklin was able to get more physically and mentally out of his players.

In Tarkenton's mind, however, Van Brocklin was excessive in his criticism. He would call his players stupid, ungrateful, cowardly, slothful (lazy), selfish, and complacent.

Tarkenton prepares to make a pass during a game against the Chicago Bears. It was against the Bears that Tarkenton made his sensational debut—throwing four touchdowns and taking one in himself.

Klobuchar writes in *Tarkenton*: "As a man capable of roiling his ballplayers' juices, Van Brocklin stands almost unique. The hatreds he generated were real . . . But while his ballplayers hated or feared him much of the time, they followed him just as intensely. He was, and is, a man of worth and intelligence. For the better part of five seasons he gave the Minnesota Vikings the kind of coaching performance that . . . might not have been equaled by any other coach in football."

Like many other people, Van Brocklin's weaknesses could also reveal his strengths. His love of the game and his passion for winning created a "now or never" attitude that propelled his team toward success. He knew they were underdogs and he wanted to make top dogs out of them. They responded by working hard.

But intimidation tactics only work for so long. Sooner or later, players become bored or resentful and turn their attitudes against their coach. A believer in a gentler coaching approach, Tarkenton advises in *Tarkenton*, "You can lead a man and instruct him without having to dominate his life." Van Brocklin's plan to drive his men to greater heights of performance by breaking their confidence backfired, and he lost control of his players.

The relationship between players and coaches is one of the most fragile, yet crucial, in professional sports. Victories depend on players following the game plans of their coaches. If they lack confidence in or feel ridiculed by their coaches, those plans will never succeed—however brilliant.

Because Tarkenton had a strong sense of who he was and what he could accomplish, he did not let the Dutchman's comments get to him. He used what he could of his coach's strengths and found little time to dwell on the weaknesses. Tarkenton had a team to lead, a career to build, and a desire to win.

"Whatever the reasons," reflects Tarkenton in *Tarkenton*, "I acquired a hard skin early. And the Dutchman was part of that process. I think a quarterback has got to be a fighter. There are so many people taking shots at you, on the field, in the grandstand, in the newspapers, that you have to block all of that out and fight your way through."

Through all the badgering and humiliation, Tarkenton has maintained the philosophy that life is good, people are good, you should expect to get only what you give in life, and being negative can be very harmful. Tarkenton stuck to his beliefs. He used his scrambling style when necessary and accepted fair criticism (as the previous passage from *Tarkenton* shows) from Van Brocklin when it was appropriate.

Many fans and critics thought Tarkenton's football style of those first Vikings years was rehearsed, but Tarkenton disagrees. He has said repeatedly that he only called a scramble play once during that time. In most cases, he was simply doing whatever he could to keep the ball alive.

The Legendary Green Bay Packers

Up to that time, the Vikings franchise had yet to beat the Green Bay Packers, a team Tarkenton held in the highest regard. During a division showdown in 1964, on a desperate fourth down and 22 yards at the Vikings' thirty-five yard line, Tarkenton read the Packers prevent defense. The Packers dropped most of the protection deep to protect their lead. With nothing in the playbook for that situation, Tarkenton improvised. He told all his receivers to run about twenty-five yards, turn, and look. His plan was to run around until he found somebody to connect with.

It was hardly a sophisticated call. The Packer defense came at him. Tarkenton faked a

Under coach Vince Lombardi, the Green Bay Packers were the most successful football team of the 1960s. They won the first two Super Bowl Championships in 1967 and 1968.

deep drop into the backfield, then headed for the sidelines and turned toward the other. Willie Davis of the Packers was so close, Tarkenton could feel him. Davis took a swipe, missed him, and Tarkenton looked downfield.

He saw a receiver, Tom Hall, wide open on the Packers' 25-yard line. He hurled the ball. At that moment, Gordy Smith, the Vikings tight end, saw his quarterback throw. In a clutch play, he intercepted the ball (from his own teammate), made the catch, and ran for ten more yards out of bounds. Freddie Cox, the great Vikings kicker, made the field goal, and the Vikings won.

They had beaten the legendary head coach Vince Lombardi and the Green Bay Packers. The Packers were the Vikings' interdivision rivals. They were also famous for their tough, hard-hitting play. In fact, the Chicago Bears, the Detroit Lions, and the Packers were together known as the Black and Blue Division. The Vikings were no longer upstarts. They were contenders.

Eager for a Championship

The Vikings' record steadily improved in the five years Tarkenton was on the roster. In 1964, the team's fourth season, they won more games than they lost. In 1965, bolstered by excellent recruiting and a solid force of returning veterans, they fielded what many considered their most talented team. After a successful preseason that revealed an explosive offense (they scored 57 points against the Dallas Cowboys), they began with high hopes, eager for a championship.

Facing the Baltimore Colts in the season opener, the Vikings melted under an unseasonable heat wave. Ninety-five degrees and high humidity drained the Vikings. They lost by three touchdowns. Another defeat in Detroit against the Lions, in the last minute, did little to rebuild their confidence. As ambitious as their offense was, the Vikings defense did little to turn any heads. Despite the weak defense, the Vikings had a 5-3 record when they faced the Colts again, this time at home in Bloomington, Minnesota.

Again their hopes were high. Johnny Unitas, the Hall of Fame quarterback for the Colts, was ailing, and the Colts second-string quarterback, Gary Cuozzo, did not threaten the Vikings. They should have given him more credit. Cuozzo burned the weak Viking defense for five touchdowns and a humiliating home defeat. Van Brocklin shocked everyone, including his team, by announcing his resignation the next morning.

Jim Finks, the general manager of the Vikings, hoped Van Brocklin would reconsider

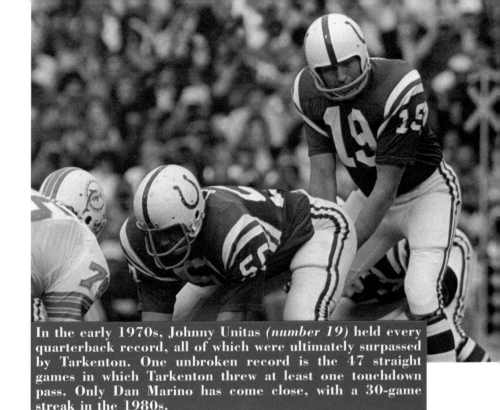

In the early 1970s, Johnny Unitas *(number 19)* held every quarterback record, all of which were ultimately surpassed by Tarkenton. One unbroken record is the 47 straight games in which Tarkenton threw at least one touchdown pass. Only Dan Marino has come close, with a 30-game streak in the 1980s.

his decision. Tarkenton was disappointed that a coach who had preached the importance of perseverance was now quitting because of a loss. Like many of the other players, Tarkenton lost faith in his coach. The next day, Van Brocklin returned, but the Viking atmosphere would never be the same. The season ended with a 7-7 record. The next season would be Tarkenton's last in Minnesota.

Belonging
with the Best

The 1966 season was one of ups and downs for Fran Tarkenton and the Minnesota Vikings. The team ended the season with a miserable 4-9-1 record. What were the ups? The Vikings beat Vince Lombardi's Green Bay Packers, who were a standard they measured themselves against. And why not? The Packer dynasty of the 1960s was about to peak, and beating the Packers with drives called by Tarkenton felt about as good as it could get.

Around the league, Tarkenton was held in high regard. But plenty of people resented his style. Had he not been a scrambling quarterback, had he just stayed in the pocket and taken the hard hits, some coaches, fans, and commentators might not have had a problem

Tarkenton practices during spring training after being traded to the New York Giants in 1967.

with him. But Tarkenton did not play like other quarterbacks, who always stayed close to the line of scrimmage. He did not get the respect that quarterbacks like Johnny Unitas and Bart Starr got, simply because he was willing to leave the pocket.

Players could appreciate what Tarkenton was doing, however. They understood that he was not being cowardly by leaving the pocket. He was trying to find the best or only way possible to help his team. And if that meant that he could avoid the pain of a 250-pound lineman crashing against his bones, so be it.

The Pro Bowl quarterbacks Sonny Jurgensen, Bart Starr, and Johnny Unitas were cut from a classic quarterback mold. As if to punish Tarkenton for not fitting into that mold, even when he threw five interceptions after the 1966 victory against Green Bay, Van Brocklin chose to start his other quarterbacks and leave Tarkenton on the bench. In the Dutchman's mind, the season was already over, and he had begun working toward the next season. Jim Finks, the general manager, had similar

Bart Starr of the Green Bay Packers emerged as one of the best quarterbacks in the NFL. He led his team to five NFL titles and two Super Bowl victories. A 17th round draft pick (200th overall) in 1956, he was enshrined in the Hall of Fame in 1977.

thoughts and decided an overhaul of the Vikings was in order. Gone would be both Tarkenton and Van Brocklin, and a new era for the Vikings would begin.

Tarkenton knew this would be the right move. His achievements in Minnesota were great enough that he wouldn't have trouble being picked up by another team. He sent a letter of resignation to the Vikings, clearly stating his desire to be traded. They agreed.

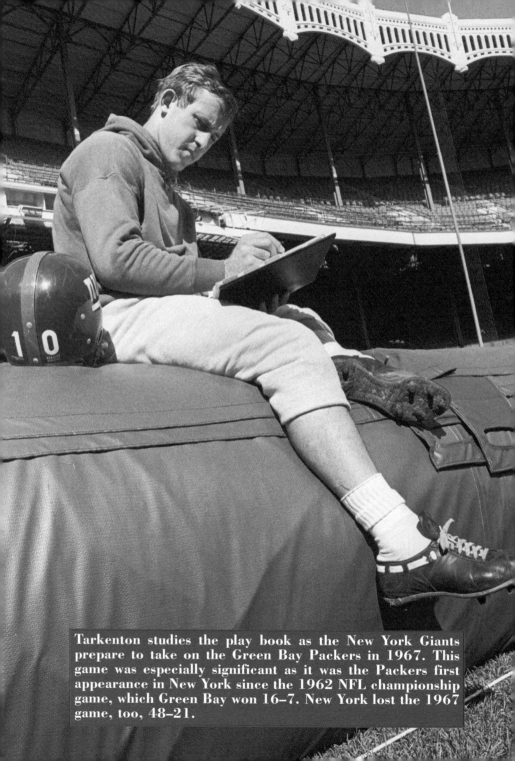

Tarkenton studies the play book as the New York Giants prepare to take on the Green Bay Packers in 1967. This game was especially significant as it was the Packers first appearance in New York since the 1962 NFL championship game, which Green Bay won 16–7. New York lost the 1967 game, too, 48–21.

Planning for His Future

The New York Giants were looking for a quarter-back who could throw touchdowns. Their team had been steadily disintegrating, and a rebuilding phase had begun. They were willing to give away a few draft picks in order to get Scramblin' Fran Tarkenton. At the very least, they knew he would bring some excitement back into their game. Tarkenton would find a new home and a whole new life in New York.

Tarkenton had graduated from college with a degree in business. Unlike many other professional athletes, he knew that his playing days would eventually end. In those days, football players did not make the enormous sums of money players command today. The majority made less than $20,000 a year in the late 1960s. Today, football players earn that amount for a single game.

In the 1960s, pro football players had to have other jobs to supplement the income they earned playing the game. Tarkenton was a rule-breaker in this regard as well. He was wary of the "spend now, worry later" attitude that most football players had, and he decided to go against the grain.

Even today, people are eager to invite football players to fancy dinners, take them to golf courses, and give them the illusion that the high-style life will last forever. But many players are left with little when their careers are through. Their bodies have been punished by the violent sport, and because few take their education seriously they often do not have other careers to fall back on. If they last long in the game, they begin new lives at the ages of thirty to thirty-five. The player gets a retirement dinner, a couple of interviews on television, and perhaps a few speaking engagements. But fairly soon, the public and the fans have their eyes fixed upon the new rising talents. Yesterday's football heroes quickly vanish. The once-admired quarterback, running back, or defensive end is now a has-been.

Tarkenton was smarter than that. He saw through the illusion and secured a financial future for his family, regardless of what monies he earned playing football. He vowed he would not fade into history. Putting his ego aside and putting his brain in gear, Tarkenton decided to use all his business sense while he was still playing football. And his new home, New York, was the perfect city in which to test his business abilities. His business philosophy then and now is simple, direct, and stated clearly in *Tarkenton.* "I'm a capitalist without apology. I believe the so-called work ethic can be distorted, but by and large it is very defensible and very much at the heart of what makes a country like the United States an exciting place . . . I am not obsessed by money. But I don't find the making of money sinister or irrelevant when it is a reward for effort, risk, legitimate capitalization, or ingenuity. A long time ago I decided I wanted several sources of income, some of them not related to football, and none of them dependent upon each other. This would broaden my life and make me less vulnerable to the accidents and flukes of a football career."

Tarkenton feels that athletes should not allow themselves to believe that the best days are over when an athletic career ends. With proper planning and a healthy attitude, the years following a professional sports career can be equally rewarding.

Playing for the Giants

In New York, Tarkenton practiced what he preached, both on the field and off. He enjoyed the energy of New York City and the Giants fans. Tarkenton recalls with admiration and affection the fans' devotion to the game and the players in *Tarkenton*. "They are as memorable in some ways as the ball games. I think the New York fans are more demonstrative than any fans I ever played for. If you do anything worthwhile, they shake the stadium with noise and their appreciation. You can't walk down the street during a football season and accept the stock portrait of New York as a coldhearted town. Truck drivers and garbage collectors yell to you, 'Hey, man, we're with you Sunday.'"

When Tarkenton was traded to the Giants, they needed him. Having won only one of their games the previous season, team spirit and fan morale was quite low. The Giants were not used

Tarkenton welcomed his transfer to the New York Giants, hoping to improve his play and rebuild a faltering team. In spite of his best efforts, it was not to be.

to losing—they had dominated the Eastern Conference for the first half of the 1960s. Invigorated by the new city and team and the hope of winning a championship, Tarkenton accepted the challenge as he had all previous ones. "For athletes," writes the scrambler in *Tarkenton*, "the challenge is the thing. Sure, we play for the money. But there's also the challenge to go out there and test yourself. To play for a winner is not only personal satisfaction. It is personal pride."

In his five seasons with the Giants, Tarkenton would need his personal pride. The team was in shambles when he arrived, and rebuilding was the order of the day. Despite his amazing performances, including throwing for 29 touchdowns in his first season, the losses outnumbered the wins overall. He came into New York with an outstanding contract ($50,000 a year), and he was earning $125,000 when he left. His reputation as a scrambler remained a blessing. In addition, he perfected his abilities to read defenses in a split second and complete throws that should not have been. He also continued to avoid being manhandled by monstrous linemen.

In New York, Tarkenton learned to be more of a technician as a quarterback. His coach, Allie Sherman, approached his directing of Tarkenton's natural abilities with intelligence. But even though Sherman had great regular season records, he could not lead his teams to victories in the finals. Even so, Sherman's sense of compassion and decency lingered with Tarkenton long after both had left the Giants.

Playing in the shadow of their legendary rivals, the New York Jets, the bumbling Giants were exposed in all their weakness. During one disastrous matchup, the Giants fell behind by four touchdowns within the first twenty minutes of the game. Incredibly, the Giants could not manage to field the proper number of players six times in the game—shorting themselves on each occasion.

Alex Webster assumed the reigns of command when the ax fell on Sherman. The dual 7-7 seasons in 1967 and 1968 were more than the players and fans could have or should have hoped for, but the success was not enough to save Sherman's job.

Tarkenton discusses a play with Giants head coach Alexander (Allie) Sherman. In each of his first three years (1961–1963), Sherman took the Giants to the NFL championships. Though the Giants lost all three times, twice to the Packers and once to the Bears, Sherman was named NFL Coach of the Year in 1961 and 1962, the first time such an honor was awarded to the same person in consecutive years.

The 1969 season began on a promising note. The opening game matched the Giants against Tarkenton's old team, the Vikings. Tarkenton was running the entire game, trying desperately not to get eaten by a now-legendary Viking defense. Tarkenton found his only salvage of the game in being able to hand the ball off. On one memorable play, Tarkenton, scrambling for his life with no view of his receivers, heaved the ball downfield. It flew 55 yards downfield to the two Vikings defensive backs. They swatted the ball away, and it landed on Butch Wilson, the Giants' only receiver, who lay flat on his back. In reflex, Wilson completed the pass. Shaken by the miraculous play, the Viking defense crumbled. Tarkenton went on to complete two touchdown passes, one in the game's final minute. The Giants beat the Vikings 24–23.

The Giants won three of their first four games of the 1969 season. It looked like they would no longer be the doormats of the NFL. But luck left them after that. Their new offensive schemes were easily read by defenses. They finished the season 6-8.

Tarkenton's next season in New York produced nine wins. Greg Larson, the center for the Giants, credited Tarkenton for all the team's success. Tarkenton became a celebrity. His face appeared on Wheaties cereal boxes. His business interests were doing well, and the Giants appeared to be headed for something greater. They had come within one game of the playoffs. Tarkenton's scrambling was no longer a point of ridicule. In fact, other pro quarterbacks were starting to imitate his moves on the field.

He also got involved in a contract dispute with the Giants. Tarkenton was not entirely happy with his salary in New York. He proposed a different payment schedule, which would pay him a smaller yearly salary and reduce the amount of taxes he would have to pay, but which would extend his contract three years. The Giants didn't go for the idea. Tarkenton missed an exhibition game because of the breakdown in negotiations.

The media had a field day with Tarkenton's behavior, though they did not know the whole story. They mistakenly believed he had become selfish and reveled too much in his celebrity status. "If we choose popularity as a criterion of everything we do, we are going to frustrate ourselves into a very dark corner, or wind up as cheerleaders for people we call our betters," he writes in *Tarkenton*. "I just have a hard time accepting that kind of behavior." Tarkenton would not bow to the demands of the management because he felt he had offered them a very fair deal. Bonus arrangements and personal goals aside, Tarkenton was not about to lose control of his career.

Injuries and loss of concentration plagued the team. The highlight for Tarkenton that year was defeating the Atlanta Falcons, who were led by his former coach, Norm Van Brocklin. In the game against the Falcons, Tarkenton wisely controlled the clock. In the final seconds, he opted out of the called pass play and ran the ball in himself, winning the game.

But seasons are not made by one game or one player. With a final record of 4-10, Tarkenton considered his position. He knew that he was the property of the New York Giants. But he also knew that, if he was unhappy or performing poorly, he could be traded to another team. A month after the season ended, Tarkenton called the Giants management. They had been talking with the Vikings and wondered how Tarkenton would feel about playing with his old team again. Though he had to take a cut in pay, the Vikings gave him back his number 10 jersey. A new era was about to begin in Minnesota.

You Can't Go Home Again

6

T he Minnesota Vikings were not the same team Tarkenton had left in the mid 1960s. Bud Grant, the new head coach, had led them to four consecutive Central Division titles on the success of the now legendary Purple People Eater defense.

Consisting of Alan Page (1971's Most Valuable Player in the NFL), Carl Eller, Gary Larsen, and Jim Marshall, the defense's motto, "Meet at the quarterback," helped establish them as one of the most dominant defenses in football history.

Quarterbacks feared them even though none of them weighed more than 250 pounds; they played like men twice their size with double the speed. They smashed through offensive lines, pounding quarterbacks and halfbacks

Minnesota Vikings coach Bud Grant, the eighth winningest coach in NFL history. In his second year Grant took the team on a stretch in which they won 11 division titles in 13 years, the NFL championship in 1969, and three NFC titles.

alike. They blocked field goals and caused fumbles. Though they averaged 37 sacks per season, they put more pressure on offenses than those numbers reveal. And Alan Page, for one, was not certain that the presence of Fran Tarkenton would miraculously grant the Vikings a much-coveted Super Bowl title. Bud Grant and the Minnesota faithful thought otherwise.

Tarkenton's return to Minnesota was not unlike a hero's return after a war. He came to Minnesota to provide stability in the quarterback position and was greeted not only by fans, but commercial interests as well. He would become an advertising darling, starring in a savings and loan commercial little more than twenty-four hours after he arrived back in Minnesota. Tarkenton signed on for commercial endorsements at a time when few professional football players received such exposure. Those who did were often subject to ridicule or considered by their peers to be less-than-serious about football. Tarkenton's commercials would flood the television airwaves, causing him some embarrassment. He did not want that kind of overexposure, even though his business sensibilities encouraged him to seek profit wherever he could find it.

It was that same sense of adventure that had helped to create his image of being a scrambler, and though Tarkenton had no plans of dissolving the image of Scramblin' Fran, the Minnesota offensive line would allow him to become an even greater quarterback. Tarkenton insisted he was not in Minnesota as a savior. All the pieces of the puzzle were there—he would be the man to help put it together.

In his first season back in Minnesota, he did not put it together. The 1972 Vikings finished 7-7, but hardly anyone who knew football would blame Tarkenton for the disappointing record. There were key injuries, missed field goals, crucial fumbles, and numerous mental errors.

But Tarkenton didn't accept excuses. He took full responsibility for the Vikings' performance. Tarkenton recalls in *Tarkenton* that, when he won the team award for the Most Valuable Player, he said, "I'm the quarterback who was supposed to provide leadership, help this team win the Super Bowl. I don't want to belittle the award, but the only award that's meaningful is the one they give after the Super Bowl. This has to be my biggest disappointment after a lot of disappointments."

The 7-7 record and his perception of being only half a winner haunted Tarkenton. In a self-critical way, it spoke to him of his own mediocrity, his own personal failure. His head

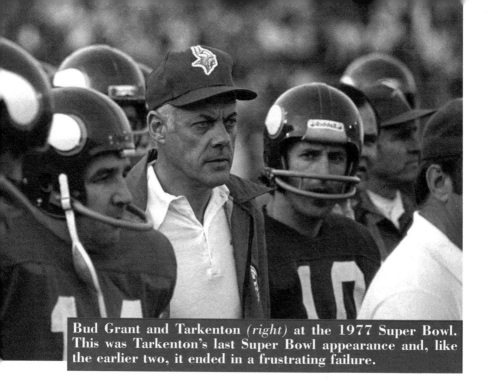

Bud Grant and Tarkenton *(right)* at the 1977 Super Bowl. This was Tarkenton's last Super Bowl appearance and, like the earlier two, it ended in a frustrating failure.

coach, Bud Grant, helped him put the record into perspective. Grant's philosophy was that, even though the quarterback called the plays and threw the passes, he was no more responsible for winning or losing than any other player. As the most visible member of the team, the quarterback often gets credit for a victory or blamed for a defeat. But a football game is a team effort. No single member can win or lose on his own.

Tarkenton characterized Grant as a man who was untouched by the violence and passion of the game around him. Grant kept his head in the game, commanding the players with a kind of military discipline and an air of professionalism. He challenged his players to be consistent, focused, and in control. At practices, Grant was quite different from his public image. Tarkenton recalls a lack of tension and a lot of laughter. He never tried to humiliate a player, and he approached each player with respect. If a player could not follow instructions, or if he simply was not talented enough, he would no longer be allowed to play for the Minnesota Vikings. The players trusted Grant, believed in what he coached, and followed his wisdom. Tarkenton would have to remember Grant's wisdom in the seasons to follow.

The Ultimate

The 1973 season for the Minnesota Vikings took them to their second Super Bowl. What had not worked the season before had finally fallen into place. The Vikings swept the preseason and then won nine games in a row before suffering a defeat to Norm Van Brocklin's Atlanta Falcons.

That defeat was not enough to deflate the Vikings. "For the first time in Tarkenton's professional life it all blended: the fraternity of the field and dressing room, the burgeoning excitement, the anticipation of the playoff season, the triumphant tone of the crowds. The country was watching," writes Klobuchar in *Tarkenton*. Though it had taken twelve seasons, Tarkenton finally felt justified. All the sweat and blood in his journey had been worth it.

Tarkenton admired the strength and determination of his teammates, in particular Jim Marshall, Alan Page, and Carl Eller. He was inspired by their consistent yet fierce respect for the game. By the time the Vikings faced the Cowboys in Dallas for the NFC championship, they were relaxed and ready. Their offense worked liked magic, misdirecting a Dallas defense known for its offense-crushing abilities. Tarkenton's amazing 65-yard pass seemed an appropriate symbol for the level of the entire team's play. With a final score of 21–7, the Minnesota Vikings were prepared to do what they had not yet been able to do—win a Super Bowl.

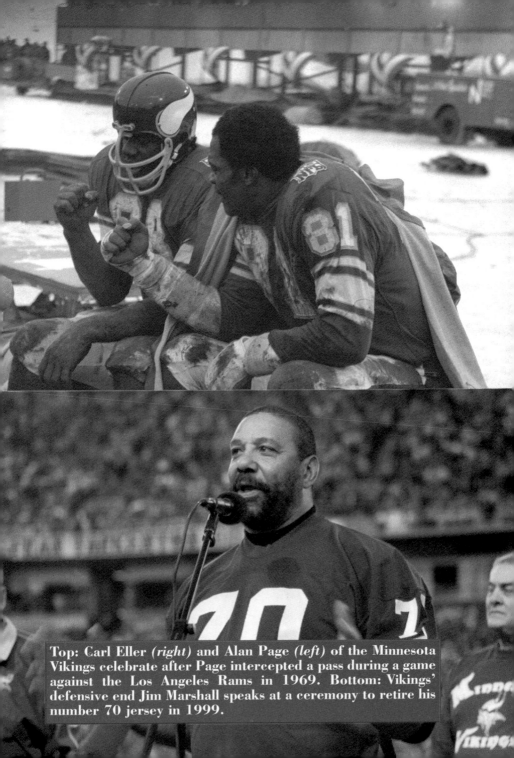

Top: Carl Eller *(right)* and Alan Page *(left)* of the Minnesota Vikings celebrate after Page intercepted a pass during a game against the Los Angeles Rams in 1969. Bottom: Vikings' defensive end Jim Marshall speaks at a ceremony to retire his number 70 jersey in 1999.

The Super Bowl is the height of a football player's career. It reveals all of a player's passion and confirms his place among the elite of professional football. Rarely are players ever prepared for the spectacle. The pressure, personally and professionally, breaks some of them. The entire nation focuses on these players, increasing the pressure and creating a carnival of distractions.

The Minnesota Vikings triumphed over the first major distraction, one unheard of in NFL history: They had no locker room in which to prepare and dress for practice! The Vikings had been given the use of the facilities of a local school before the big game. Not only were there no lockers, only three of the fifteen showers actually worked. Sparrows nested in the school's ceiling. Uncharacteristically, Bud Grant exploded. At their first press conference in Houston, he berated the NFL for this oversight. Facing fines from Commissioner Pete Rozelle, Grant regained his composure and explained how degrading the situation was to his players and the dignity of the Super Bowl. It was not enough—he was fined anyway.

Tarkenton accepted it all, and in an interview recalled in *Tarkenton*, revealed his thoughts about the big game: "I've never been so hungry, and I've never been with a team I thought was so ready."

The Vikings took the field against the Miami Dolphins in Super Bowl VIII inspired and unwilling to accept even the idea of defeat. They were soon deflated. Miami scored on its opening drive, and then again five minutes later. By the second quarter, Miami was ahead 17–0. Bob Griese, Larry Czonka, and the rest of the Miami offense confused the Viking defense. The Miami defense had shut down the powerful Minnesota offense. Tarkenton took command. He led the Vikings' first successful drive, only to have it fumbled by Oscar Reed.

The second half of the game was no better. The Vikings managed one touchdown, scored by Tarkenton, and went away with a 24–7 loss. Even though Tarkenton had set a Super Bowl record for accuracy in passing, he felt little pride. "We were belted," he says in *Tarkenton*, "but it wasn't the kind of defeat that embarrassed you.

You felt drained and deflated. You know you've gotten that far, and then it's over . . . All of a sudden nobody seems to remember the kind of season your team had, the challenges it handled, the peaks it achieved."

Tarkenton walked off the field with Grady Alderman, who had been his teammate back in 1961. They were the only remnants of the original Minnesota Vikings. Who would have thought they'd come this far? Yet their journey was not over.

Another Chance

The 1974 season began anxiously for Tarkenton because for the first time in his career, an injury was forcing him to play in pain. Though he was self-conscious about it, Tarkenton kept his worries to himself. After all, the Vikings were having a winning season and the public knew little about the injury. The Vikings won 11 games and defeated the Los Angeles Rams for the NFC championship in one of the most brutal games the Vikings had ever played. Though in pain, Tarkenton was still a force to be reckoned with.

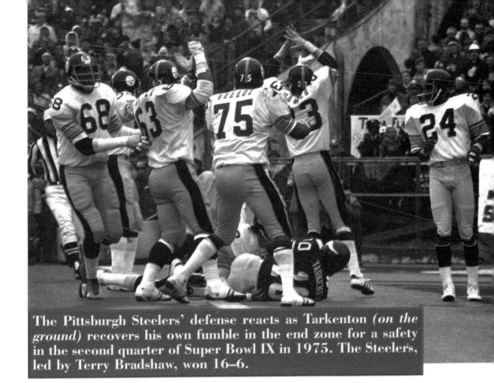

The Pittsburgh Steelers' defense reacts as Tarkenton *(on the ground)* recovers his own fumble in the end zone for a safety in the second quarter of Super Bowl IX in 1975. The Steelers, led by Terry Bradshaw, won 16–6.

The 1975 Super Bowl pitted the Vikings against the Pittsburgh Steelers' Terry Bradshaw, Franco Harris, Mean Joe Greene, L. C. Greenwood, Jack Lambert, Jack Ham, and their infamous defense, known as the Steel Curtain. The Steel Curtain came down hard on the Vikings, batting away Tarkenton's passes like badminton birdies, and allowing the Viking offense only six points. The 16–6 loss in Super Bowl IX was heartbreaking. Two consecutive Super Bowl appearances, and two consecutive losses. How would Tarkenton recover?

In the off-season, Tarkenton worked on rehabilitating his throwing arm. He visited the anatomy department at Michigan State University, and after learning about muscular structure, realized the seriousness of his injury. In order to maintain his career, Tarkenton would have to become even more durable. Coach Bud Grant had told Tarkenton that durability was probably the most important quality in a football player. "It's one of the principal reasons Francis has become the greatest quarterback in pro football history," Grant is quoted as saying in *Tarkenton*.

The Vikings team physician, Dr. Don Lannin, marveled at Tarkenton's reflexes and ability to see the field, but he also worried about Tarkenton's lack of fear when taking hits by giant linemen. "The first down is more important to him than possible injury," Lannin said in *Tarkenton*. "If he's heading for it and it's close, he'll expose himself to the full impact of an open-field tackle. He chews out pass receivers all the time for making their cut a half-yard short of a first down."

Though the Vikings did not make it to the playoffs that season, Tarkenton did recover from his injuries. But he became a different kind of quarterback. Heading into the 1975 season, Tarkenton's abilities as a player were as sharp as ever, and he started becoming more of a consultant on the offense. He made suggestions to the coaches about where and how players might better perform. Bud Grant has said that if someone were to observe Tarkenton at a practice they might see that Tarkenton spoke with everyone on the field, including coaches, trainers, ballboys, and water boys. "This fellow really fills out his life with something meaningful almost every moment," Grant is quoted as saying in *Tarkenton*. "He involves himself. He cares what happens to his teammates, in football and outside of it . . . He seems to be a man totally adjusted and excited about the way his life is going."

Off the field, Tarkenton was also known for his generosity, giving away his 1974 Super Bowl salary to the needy. As much as he took care of himself as a football player, he took pride in his

Fran Tarkenton looks dejected after his third Super Bowl bid ends in defeat. Tarkenton and Miami Dolphins' quarterback Dan Marino will be remembered as two of the greatest quarterbacks never to win a Super Bowl ring.

role as father to Angela, Matthew, and Melissa and as husband to Elaine, never forgetting the deep importance of family in his life.

On the field, Grant praised Tarkenton's instincts and composure under pressure. Tarkenton's instincts led the Vikings to Super Bowl XI against the Oakland Raiders. With a 12-2 season record and 25 touchdown passes, Tarkenton was poised to make this his game. The Vikings lost the game 32–14, which was bad enough. To make matters worse, Tarkenton's beloved father, Dallas, passed away in Georgia while watching the game.

The Depth
of Loss

How does one measure the depth of loss? His father's death was certainly one of the more painful events in Fran Tarkenton's life. Gathering his family together he flew east for the funeral. Such times call for self-evaluation, a review of priorities, accomplishments, and future goals.

A principle his father had preached his whole life, the basic goodness of people, showed itself during Tarkenton's grieving period. Celebrities and noncelebrities from across the country—many who had not even known Dallas Tarkenton—sent their best wishes and gifts for the memorial fund. Many made appearances at the funeral. Tarkenton was quite proud of his father, both as a minister to humanity and as a loving family man. When Tarkenton spoke at his father's graveside he reminded those present to take the time to tell others how they felt about them, and how important they are to them. He took notice of his old college coach, Quinton Lumpkin, and let him know how much he appreciated the coach's belief in him.

Tarkenton says in *What Losing Taught Me About Winning*, a guide to success in small and home-based businesses, that he never felt defeated by his final Super Bowl loss, or by any other. "Within a few hours of each of those losses, I was ready to get back into the fight again. I never questioned my worthiness to be in the game." Until 1993, when Jim Kelly, quarterback for the Buffalo Bills, lost four Super Bowls, Tarkenton held the record as the quarterback who had lost more Super Bowls than any other.

Does this make Tarkenton a failure? He was the hard worker who could not get a Super Bowl ring. He was the quarterback who could not lead his team to the ultimate victory. But the only thing that makes a person a loser, Tarkenton says, is to accept the name and to be a quitter. "The only

Buffalo Bills quarterback Jim Kelly groans after losing Super Bowl XXVI to the Washington Redskins. With this fourth loss, Kelly broke Tarkenton's record of three Super Bowl losses.

way you can become a 'failure' is to accept failure as a finality," he writes in *What Losing Taught Me About Winning.* "When you are feeling angry or hurt, it is a tremendous energy force, and you have to choose whether to use that energy in a negative fashion or to do something productive that creates value for others. By choosing the positive outlet, your life will change for the better."

The Scrambler Retires

Fran Tarkenton ended his professional football career in 1978, playing in the first 16-game

Fran Tarkenton Career Statistics

Passing

246 Games
6,467 Attempts
3,686 Completions
57 Percentage
47,003 Yards
342 Touchdowns
266 Interceptions
80.4 Rating

Rushing

246 Games
675 Attempts
3,674 Yards
5.4 Average
32 Touchdowns

schedule in the NFL. He threw for nearly 3,500 yards passing and 25 touchdowns. He led the Vikings to the Central Division Championship. Injuries certainly contributed to Tarkenton's decision to quit playing. But more than that, Tarkenton had enjoyed a brilliant and satisfactory career. It is rare to find players who last—physically and mentally—as long as Tarkenton did. And when he left the game, he was the NFL's all-time leader in numerous quarterback passing statistics.

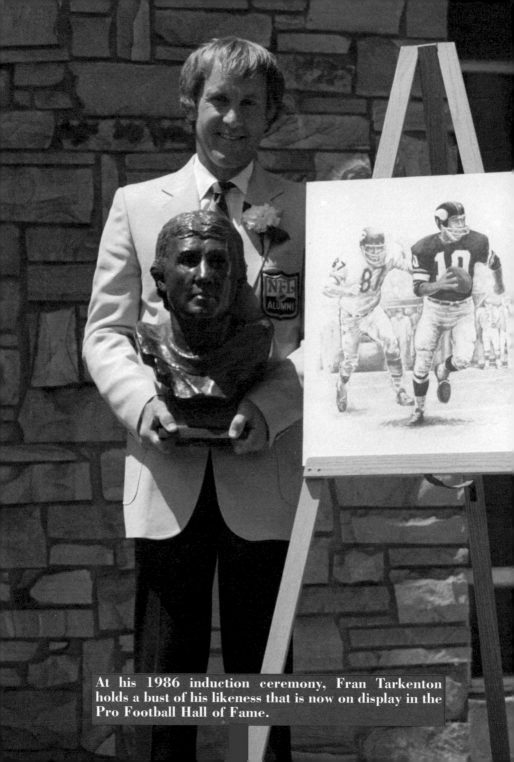

At his 1986 induction ceremony, Fran Tarkenton holds a bust of his likeness that is now on display in the Pro Football Hall of Fame.

On August 2, 1986, Fran Tarkenton was inducted into the NFL Hall of Fame in Canton, Ohio. He was the first Minnesota Vikings player to win the honor. His induction reinforced all his accomplishments as a Viking, a New York Giant, and as a football player. Of his status as a Hall of Famer, Tarkenton says in *What Losing Taught Me About Winning*, "I am in the Hall of Fame because I overcame my physical limitations and became a pretty fair player through determination, hard work, and a hard-earned understanding of how to play the game."

In the end, it would be nearly impossible to label this catch-me-if-you-can Hall of Famer as a failure or a loser. Instead, he has taken the curves life has thrown at him, caught them, and thrown back for immense gains. Sometimes in life, one has to scramble. Tarkenton did not fit the mold of an NFL quarterback. But by breaking the right rules he scrambled his way into NFL history. By all accounts—as a family man, businessman, author, motivational speaker, trailblazer, and NFL Hall of Fame quarterback—Fran Tarkenton is a winner.

Timeline

1940 Francis Asbury Tarkenton is born in Richmond, Virginia.

1945 The Tarkenton family moves to Washington, D.C.

1956–1957 As a high school football player, Tarkenton leads his team at Athens High School (Georgia) to a state championship; he is selected to all-state teams in football, baseball, and basketball.

1957 Tarkenton leads freshmen Georgia team to an unbeaten season and is selected for the All-SEC freshmen team.

1958 Selected for the All-SEC sophomore team.

1959 Leads University of Georgia to unbeaten season, SEC Championship, and Orange Bowl victory.

1960 Leads SEC in total offense yards, passing; selected for All-American Second Team; selected for All-American Academic First Team.

1961 Drafted by the Minnesota Vikings; in his first regular season game appearance throws four TD passes and rushes for another; finishes second in Rookie of the Year voting.

1964 First Pro Bowl appearance; named MVP of Pro Bowl.

1965 Second Pro Bowl appearance.

Tarkenton, holding the ball, in action in a 1971 game against the St. Louis Cardinals when he was with the New York Giants.

1967 Traded to the New York Giants.

1972 Returns to Minnesota Vikings; named All-NFC by the United Press International and *Sporting News.*

1973 Vikings win NFC Central Championship, play in Super Bowl VIII against Miami Dolphins, but lose 24–7; Tarkenton named All-Pro selection.

1974 Vikings repeat NFC Central Championship, play in Super Bowl IX against Pittsburgh Steelers (lose 16–6).

1975 Vikings win NFC Central Championship; Tarkenton named NFL Most Valuable Player by Associated Press, *Sporting News*, Newspaper Enterprise Association, and *Pro Football Weekly.*

1976 Vikings win fourth consecutive NFC Central Championship, play in Super Bowl XI against Oakland Raiders (lose 32–14); Tarkenton is selected to Pro Bowl—does not play; misses first professional start due to injury.

1978 Tarkenton's final season. Leads Vikings to NFC Central Championship.

1986 Inducted into the NFL Hall of Fame in Canton, Ohio.

Glossary

capitalist A person who believes in an economic system characterized by private ownership of goods.

complacent Content to the point of being unconcerned.

completion A forward pass that is caught by the thrower's teammate.

drive The series of plays a team puts together in an attempt to score.

elusive Difficult to grasp.

end zone The area beyond the goal line.

evangelical Emphasizing the salvation of the soul through Christian gospels.

expansion team A new team in the NFL.

first down The first chance out of four that a team on offense has to advance ten yards.

formidable Causing fear or dread.

franchise Membership rights in a professional team.

fumble The accidental or caused dropping of the ball.

line of scrimmage An imaginary line that marks the position of the ball.

pocket The area of protection for a quarterback formed by his blockers.

prevent defense A defensive play designed to deny the offense a high yardage pass.

punt When a player ten yards behind the center catches a snap, drops it, and kicks it before it hits the ground; an opponent tries to catch and advance it in the other direction.

receiver An offensive player who catches or attempts to catch a forward pass.

rush A running pass.

sack The tackling of the quarterback behind the line of scrimmage while he is trying to pass.

scheme An arrangement of players.

series The group of four downs a team has in which to advance ten yards.

For More Information

College Football Hall of Fame
111 South St. Joseph Street
South Bend, IN 46601
(800) 440-FAME (440-3263)
Web site: http://www.collegefootball.org

National Football League
280 Park Avenue
New York, NY 10017
Web site: http://www.nfl.com

The University of Georgia
Athens, GA 30602
(706) 542-3000
Web site: http://www.uga.edu

Web Sites
Due to the changing nature of Internet links, the
Rosen Publishing Group, Inc., has developed an
online list of Web sites related to the subject of this
book. This site is updated regularly. Please use this
link to access the list:

http://www.rosenlinks.com/fhf/ftar/

For Further Reading

Italia, Bob. *The Minnesota Vikings*. Edina, MN: Abdo & Daughters, 1996.

Klobuchar, Jim. *Knights and Knaves of Autumn: 40 Years of Pro Football and the Minnesota Vikings*. Cambridge, MA: Adventure Publications, 2000.

Klobuchar, Jim. *Purple Hearts and Golden Memories: 35 Years with the Minnesota Vikings*. Coal Valley, IL: Quality Sports Publications, 1995.

Klobuchar, Jim, and Fran Tarkenton. *Tarkenton*. New York: Harper & Row, 1976.

Libby, Bill. *Fran Tarkenton: The Scrambler*. New York: Putnam, 1970.

Tarkenton, Fran. *No Time for Losing*. New York: Ballantine, 1967.

Tarkenton, Fran, and Wes Smith. *What Losing Taught Me About Winning: The Ultimate Guide for Success in Small and Home-Based Businesses*. New York: Simon & Schuster, 1997.

Bibliography

Donovan, John. CNN/Sports Illustrated. "Standing
    Tall." July 28, 1998. Retrieved November 2001
    (http://sportsillustrated.cnn.com/football/nfl/
    news/1998/07/28/short_qbs/index.html).
Holden, Anthony. CBS Sportsline.com. "The
    Purple People-Eaters." Retrieved December
    2001 (http://www.sportsline.com/u/ce/feature/
    0%2C1518%2C2749886_59%2C00.html).
Klobuchar, Jim, and Fran Tarkenton. *Tarkenton*.
    New York: Harper & Row, 1976.
"Lessons and Legends," NFL's Greatest
    Moments, ESPN.
"Not How We Drew It Up." NFL's Greatest
    Moments, ESPN.
Tarkenton, Fran. *No Time for Losing*. New York:
    Ballantine, 1967.
Tarkenton, Fran, and Wes Smith. *What
    Losing Taught Me About Winning: The
    Ultimate Guide for Success in Small and
    Home-Based Businesses*. New York: Simon
    & Schuster, 1997.

Index

About the Author

David Hulm is a freelance writer, editor, and
poet who lives in Iowa City with his daughter.
On Sunday afternoons, he puts on a Green Bay
Packers jersey and plays football with friends
and family.

Photo Credits

Cover, pp. 54, 71 © Sports Chrome; pp. 4, 17,
41, 48–49, 61, 63, 65, 66, 74–75, 81, 84, 87
(top), 100, 103 © Bettmann/Corbis; p. 9 © Scott
Cunningham/Getty Images; p. 13 © James
Lemass/Index Stock Imagery; pp. 20, 24, 29, 32
© University of Georgia; pp. 36, 38, 45, 47, 58,
87 (bottom), 91, 94, 98 © AP/Wide World Pho-
tos

Series Design and Layout

Tahara Hasan